Francis Frith's

NORTHAMPTONSHIRE
LIVING MEMORIES

MARTIN ANDREW is an architectural and landscape historian and writer on
outdoor matters. He is also the Conservation Officer for Wycombe District
Council in Buckinghamshire. He specialises in the landscape of lowland
England and combines his love of history, landscape and architecture in his
writing. Since 1978 he has lived in Haddenham in Buckinghamshire with
his wife and children. The author is a keen long distance walker and enjoys
riding his classic motor cycle round the country lanes of the Chilterns. He
was born in Doncaster, and knows Northamptonshire well; besides walking
many of its footpaths and bridleways, he has written on the county's history.
After university he worked for the Greater London Council's Historic Buildings
Division, Buckinghamshire County and Salisbury District Councils before
joining Wycombe District Council in 1990.

photographs of the mid twentieth century

Francis Frith's

NORTHAMPTONSHIRE
LIVING MEMORIES

Martin Andrew

First published in the United Kingdom in 2002 by The Francis Frith Collection

Hardback Edition 2002 ISBN 1-85937-529-4

Paperback Edition 2005 ISBN 1-84589-078-7

British Library Cataloguing in Publication Data

Northamptonshire Living Memories
Martin Andrew
ISBN 1-84589-078-7

The Francis Frith Collection
Frith's Barn, Teffont,
Salisbury, Wiltshire SP3 5QP
Tel: +44 (0) 1722 716 376
Email: info@francisfrith.co.uk
www.francisfrith.co.uk

Printed and bound in Great Britain

Front Cover: Northampton, *Market Place c1950* N40011t

*The colour-tinting is for illustrative purposes only, and is not intended
to be historically accurate*

Aerial photographs reproduced under licence from
Simmons Aerofilms Limited.
Historical Ordnance Survey maps reproduced under licence from
Homecheck.co.uk

Every attempt has been made to contact copyright holders of
illustrative material. We will be happy to give full acknowledgement
in future editions for any items not credited. Any information should
be directed to The Francis Frith Collection.

AS WITH ANY HISTORICAL DATABASE THE FRITH ARCHIVE IS
CONSTANTLY BEING CORRECTED AND IMPROVED AND THE
PUBLISHERS WOULD WELCOME INFORMATION ON OMISSIONS
OR INACCURACIES

contents

Francis Frith: Victorian Pioneer

FRANCIS FRITH, Victorian founder of the world-famous photographic archive, was a complex and multi-talented man. A devout Quaker and a highly successful Victorian businessman, he was both philosophical by nature and pioneering in outlook.

By 1855 Francis Frith had already established a wholesale grocery business in Liverpool, and sold it for the astonishing sum of £200,000, which is the equivalent today of over £15,000,000. Now a very rich man, he was able to indulge his passion for travel. As a child he had pored over travel books written by early explorers, and his fancy and imagination had been stirred by family holidays to the sublime mountain regions of Wales and Scotland. 'What lands of spirit-stirring and enriching scenes and places!' he had written. He was to return to these scenes of grandeur in later years to 'recapture the thousands of vivid and tender memories', but with a different purpose. Now in his thirties, and captivated by the new science of photography, Frith set out on a series of pioneering journeys to the Nile regions that occupied him from 1856 until 1860.

Intrigue and Adventure

He took with him on his travels a specially-designed wicker carriage that acted as both dark-room and sleeping chamber. These far-flung journeys were packed with intrigue and adventure. In his life story, written when he was sixty-three, Frith tells of being held captive by bandits, and of fighting 'an awful midnight battle to the very point of surrender with a deadly pack of hungry, wild dogs'. Sporting flowing Arab costume, Frith arrived at Akaba by camel sixty years before Lawrence, where he encountered 'desert princes and rival sheikhs, blazing with jewel-hilted swords'.

During these extraordinary adventures he was assiduously exploring the desert regions bordering the Nile and patiently recording the antiquities and peoples with his camera. He was the first photographer to venture beyond the sixth cataract. Africa was still the mysterious 'Dark Continent', and Stanley and Livingstone's historic meeting was a decade into the future. The conditions for picture taking confound belief. He laboured for hours in his wicker dark-room in the sweltering heat of the desert, while the volatile chemicals fizzed dangerously in their trays. Often he was forced to work in remote tombs and caves where conditions were cooler. Back in London he exhibited his photographs and was 'rapturously cheered' by members of the Royal Society. His reputation as a photographer was made overnight. An eminent modern historian has likened their impact on the population of the time to that on our own generation of the first photographs taken on the surface of the moon.

Venture of a Life-Time

Characteristically, Frith quickly spotted the opportunity to create a new business as a specialist publisher of photographs. He lived in an era of immense and sometimes violent change. For the poor in the early part of Victoria's reign work was a drudge and the hours long, and people had precious little free time to enjoy themselves. Most had no transport other than a cart or gig at their disposal, and had not travelled far beyond the boundaries of their own town or village. However, by the 1870s, the railways had threaded their way

across the country, and Bank Holidays and half-day Saturdays had been made obligatory by Act of Parliament. All of a sudden the ordinary working man and his family were able to enjoy days out and see a little more of the world.

With characteristic business acumen, Francis Frith foresaw that these new tourists would enjoy having souvenirs to commemorate their days out. In 1860 he married Mary Ann Rosling and set out with the intention of photographing every city, town and village in Britain. For the next thirty years he travelled the country by train and by pony and trap, producing fine photographs of seaside resorts and beauty spots that were keenly bought by millions of Victorians. These prints were painstakingly pasted into family albums and pored over during the dark nights of winter, rekindling precious memories of summer excursions.

The Rise of Frith & Co

Frith's studio was soon supplying retail shops all over the country. To meet the demand he gathered about him a small team of photographers, and published the work of independent artist-photographers of the calibre of Roger Fenton and Francis Bedford. In order to gain some understanding of the scale of Frith's business one only has to look at the catalogue issued by Frith & Co in 1886: it runs to some 670 pages, listing not only many thousands of views of the British Isles but also many photographs of most European countries, and China, Japan, the USA and Canada – note the sample page shown on page 9 from the hand-written *Frith & Co* ledgers detailing pictures taken. By 1890 Frith had created the greatest specialist photographic publishing company in the world, with over 2,000 outlets – more than the

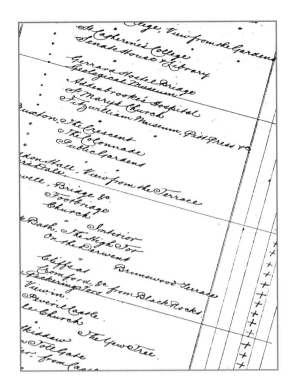

5.5 x 3.5 inches became the standard format, but it was not until 1902 that the divided back came into being, with address and message on one face and a full-size illustration on the other. *Frith & Co* were in the vanguard of postcard development, and Frith's sons Eustace and Cyril continued their father's monumental task, expanding the number of views offered to the public and recording more and more places in Britain, as the coasts and countryside were opened up to mass travel.

Francis Frith died in 1898 at his villa in Cannes, his great project still growing. The archive he created continued in business for another seventy years. By 1970 it contained over a third of a million pictures of 7,000 cities, towns and villages. The massive photographic record Frith has left to us stands as a living monument to a special and very remarkable man.

combined number that Boots and W H Smith have today! The picture on the right shows the *Frith & Co* display board at Ingleton in the Yorkshire Dales (left of window). Beautifully constructed with a mahogany frame and gilt inserts, it could display up to a dozen local scenes.

Postcard Bonanza

The ever-popular holiday postcard we know today took many years to develop. In 1870 the Post Office issued the first plain cards, with a pre-printed stamp on one face. In 1894 they allowed other publishers' cards to be sent through the mail with an attached adhesive halfpenny stamp. Demand grew rapidly, and in 1895 a new size of postcard was permitted called the court card, but there was little room for illustration. In 1899, a year after Frith's death, a new card measuring

Frith's Archive: A Unique Legacy

FRANCIS FRITH'S legacy to us today is of immense significance and value, for the magnificent archive of evocative photographs he created provides a unique record of change in 7,000 cities, towns and villages throughout Britain over a century and more. Frith and his fellow studio photographers revisited locations many times down the years to update their views, compiling for us an enthralling and colourful pageant of British life and character.

We tend to think of Frith's sepia views of Britain as nostalgic, for most of us use them to conjure up memories of places in our own lives with which we have family associations. It often makes us forget that to Francis Frith they were records of daily life as it was actually being lived in the cities, towns and villages of his day. The Victorian age was one of great and often bewildering change for ordinary people, and though the pictures evoke an impression of slower times, life was as busy and hectic as it is today.

We are fortunate that Frith was a photographer of the people, dedicated to recording the minutiae of everyday life. For it is this sheer wealth of visual data, the painstaking chronicle of changes in dress, transport, street layouts, buildings, housing, engineering and landscape that captivates us so much today. His remarkable images offer us a powerful link with the past and with the lives of our ancestors.

Today's Technology

Computers have now made it possible for Frith's many thousands of images to be accessed almost instantly. In the Frith archive today, each photograph is carefully 'digitised' then stored on a CD Rom. Frith archivists can locate a single photograph amongst thousands within seconds. Views can be catalogued and sorted under a variety of categories of place and content to the immediate benefit of researchers.

Inexpensive reference prints can be created for them at the touch of a mouse button, and a wide range of books and other printed materials assembled and published for a wider, more general readership - in the next twelve months over a hundred Frith local history titles will be published! The day-to-day workings of the archive are very different from how they were in Francis Frith's time: imagine the herculean task of sorting through eleven tons of glass negatives as Frith had to do to locate a particular sequence of pictures!

See Frith at www.francisfrith.co.uk

Yet the archive still prides itself on maintaining the same high standards of excellence laid down by Francis Frith, including the painstaking cataloguing and indexing of every view.

It is curious to reflect on how the internet now allows researchers in America and elsewhere greater instant access to the archive than Frith himself ever enjoyed. Many thousands of individual views can be called up on screen within seconds on one of the Frith internet sites, enabling people living continents away to revisit the streets of their ancestral home town, or view places in Britain where they have enjoyed holidays. Many overseas researchers welcome the chance to view special theme selections, such as transport, sports, costume and ancient monuments.

We are certain that Francis Frith would have heartily approved of these modern developments in imaging techniques, for he himself was always working at the very limits of Victorian photographic technology.

The Value of the Archive Today

Because of the benefits brought by the computer, Frith's images are increasingly studied by social historians, by researchers into genealogy and ancestory, by architects, town planners, and by teachers and schoolchildren involved in local history projects.

In addition, the archive offers every one of us an opportunity to examine the places where we and our families have lived and worked down the years. Highly successful in Frith's own era, the archive is now, a century and more on, entering a new phase of popularity.

The Past in Tune with the Future

Historians consider the Francis Frith Collection to be of prime national importance. It is the only archive of its kind remaining in private ownership and has been valued at a million pounds. However, this figure is now rapidly increasing as digital technology enables more and more people around the world to enjoy its benefits.

Francis Frith's archive is now housed in an historic timber barn in the beautiful village of Teffont in Wiltshire. Its founder would not recognize the archive office as it is today. In place of the many thousands of dusty boxes containing glass plate negatives and an all-pervading odour of photographic chemicals, there are now ranks of computer screens. He would be amazed to watch his images travelling round the world at unimaginable speeds through network and internet lines.

The archive's future is both bright and exciting. Francis Frith, with his unshakeable belief in making photographs available to the greatest number of people, would undoubtedly approve of what is being done today with his lifetime's work. His photographs, depicting our shared past, are now bringing pleasure and enlightenment to millions around the world a century and more after his death.

Northamptonshire - An Introduction

I HAVE KNOWN and loved Northamptonshire for many years and have walked what seems like the majority of its public footpaths, winding across the medieval ridge-and-furrow corrugations of its fields to visit delightful limestone or ironstone villages found clustered around their ancient medieval churches and manor houses. It is a hilly county and lies mostly along the oolitic and ironstone belts that pass through the county on their march from Dorset to Yorkshire. The county's hills, which rise above 700 ft only in a few places in its south-west, are a continuation of the Cotswolds and the ironstone hills of south Warwickshire - only without their glamour and tourist appeal. The Northamptonshire that I know is much more 'real', if you like. There is nothing to match the breathtaking perfection of Broadway or Chipping Camden, for example. Northamptonshire territory is more human and almost workaday. The county wears its architecture and beautiful and deeply historic countryside lightly and without a trace of preciousness or pretension - and it is all the better for that.

This book captures the county in the 1950s and 1960s, the latter a decade of major change that began the transformation of Northamptonshire into its present character of expanding towns and greatly improved road networks, that partly compensated for the major closures of railways. Roughly 70 miles by 20, it has long been a county through which major roads passed, radiating from London and the south heading northwards. The first such road is the Roman Watling Street, bisecting the county from Old Stratford to Lilbourne. More recently, in the late 1950s and early 1960s, came the M1 motorway that at last fully integrated Northampton into the country's main modern highway network.

The biggest development from the 1980s onwards has been the construction of east-west dual carriageways, such as the A14 and the A45. These have at last provided good cross county links, which were lacking for so much of Northamptonshire's history. The dual carriageways in effect replaced the east-west railway lines of the 1840s, which were mostly closed and dismantled in the 1960s as motor transport supplanted them. Thus the period covered by this book saw the decline of the railways and their influence on the industrial and population trends of the county. Daventry declined in the 19th century, for example, because it was not on a main railway line. By contrast, the boot and shoe industry of the Nene valley prospered due to the railway's assistance.

The 1950s were a curious twilight decade. The country still had lingering wartime rationing, austerity, drabness and relative stagnation in the early part of the decade, while by the end, the words of Prime Minister Harold Macmillan, 'You've never had it so good', echoed in its ears. In the 1960s Northamptonshire marched to the drums of progress and exciting renewal. The vogue for new towns and development corporations after the Second World War, following the New Towns Act of 1946, reached Northamptonshire in 1950. The furthest from London of the 'Mark 1' new towns, Corby, was designated in that year.

Corby, which by 1950 was the second largest town in the county, had grown up before the war around the Stewart and Lloyds steelworks. The industry exploited the local ironstone, and the settlement grew from a small village to a town of 10,000 people by 1939. The population of Corby grew to over 40,000 by 1963 and continued to expand, reaching 55,000 by 1977. Subsequent problems accompanying the decline of the steel industry came later, at a date outside the scope of this book. At the end of the 1960s the town was at the height of its optimism and its population was boosted by Glaswegian immigration. The old village is still detectable however, amid the garden suburbs, housing estates, new town centre and plethora of ring roads, new roads and roundabouts.

Next came the regeneration of the economically stagnant town of Daventry that in effect came under nearby Birmingham's influence. Like Birmingham, it wished to follow London's example of decanting industry and population outside its boundaries. A Development Corporation was set up in 1963 and Daventry was rapidly transformed from a sleeping market town of about 6,000 people into one of about 15,000. There was extensive rebuilding in the town centre and new roads added further divisions, but the old town is still 'readable' and the High Street and Market Square survive relatively intact from the 1950s. Wellingborough received similar treatment, although a development corporation was never formed, and Kettering also grew markedly in size.

The biggest growth, however, was reserved for the county town of Northampton. In 1965 it was announced in parliament that Northampton, along with Peterborough and Ipswich, was to become a 'New Town' to accommodate London's overspill. Eventually, in 1968, the Northampton Development Corporation was established. A Master Plan was drawn up in 1969 and work started on new housing and industrial estates and centres, initially to the east and south of the town. The aim was to more than double Northampton's population of 120,000 by 1981. Obviously little of this development phase belongs in this book, although rapid growth was already underway before the Development Corporation had been set up. The nearby M1 put Northampton at the hub of the national road network, with direct links to London, Birmingham and the north (that is until the motorway became choked up in the 1990s).

A glance at the county's population figures in the national censuses gives a good indication of how Northamptonshire grew in the period covered by this book. In 1951 it stood at 360,000 (a growth of only 42,000 in the years since 1939). By 1961 it had grown to 398,000, or a little over 10 per cent. The 1971 the census recorded a population of 469,000, an increase of about 18 per cent over the decade. To put the figures in perspective, the population had only increased by 14,000 between 1911 and 1939.

The boot and shoe industry and the engineering industries still formed the backbone of Northamptonshire's economy, apart of course from agriculture. This book visits many of the towns and villages caught up in this trade and manufacture at a time when it was still dominant, if a little in decline. Other industry included clothing manufacture and the widespread engineering industry, particularly around Northampton. It has to be admitted that late Victorian industry was not necessarily kind to Northamptonshire's small towns and villages, but some of the factories are impressive. Notable examples in this book include the still functioning former Co-operative Wholesale Society Limited

Corset Factory in Desborough, and the British Timken engineering works at Duston. The agricultural backbone is illustrated by the splendid Victoria Mills, Whitworth Brothers' flour mills, beside the River Nene at Wellingborough, while there is industrial grandeur in the Stewart and Lloyds steel mills at Corby, a gigantic behemoth planted amid the north Northamptonshire hills.

However, the heart of Northamptonshire seems to be a rural one, with its skein of delightful mostly stone built villages, built either in the pale oolitic limestones or the rich golden brown ironstones, and sometimes a combination of both. Dotted amid these breathtaking villages are small market towns such a Oundle, perhaps the most attractive town in Northamptonshire and home to a noted public school. Country houses, manor houses and parish churches reflect the county's past and are very much a part of its present. The villages were boosted by the managerial classes and white collar workers who took on decaying houses and cottages by the score in villages ringing the towns. They then commuted to work from their rural idylls. Despite these incomers, most villages retain a greater social mix of countrymen and townsmen than in the equally attractive Cotswold villages: and even more markedly so in the 1950s and 1960s. This book is a record of a county still at peace with itself, and in many ways, a remarkably self-sufficient place, perhaps because so many people travel through Northamptonshire en route elsewhere.

It is a very fine county with great beauty and the photograph selection in this book, I hope, underlines this, although there is no attempt to portray Northamptonshire as some kind of manifestation of a 'Merrie England' rural paradise. Many of the views are of industrial towns and villages, and in my opinion, give a better overall picture of the county within living memory than similar publications with a more nostalgic account of the past. I hope you enjoy the astonishing variety of town and village vistas to be seen in this remarkable county's 580,000 acres (234,900 hectares) as much as I have revisiting old haunts and places new to me.

Between the Rivers Nene and Welland

Oundle, North Street c1955 O103035
Our journey starts in the superb stone-built town of Oundle,
nowadays a popular tourist destination and home to Oundle
School. Note the 17th-century houses on the left, with their richly
gabled mullioned bay windows. The White Lion, dated 1641,
is now part of the school. A tall Jacobean-style school building
stands to the right, while in the distance is the market place.

Oundle, St Osyths Lane c1950 O103031

This old view of St Osyths Lane includes the beautiful 14th-century spire of St Peter's Church in the distance, beyond the market place. Of the long terrace of 17th-century cottages on the right, only the former Anchor Inn remains, dated 1637 and now a private house. The rest have been replaced by the modern back wall of a stone clad Co-op supermarket. The cottages are clearly in a dilapidated condition in this 1950 view, but their loss is surely to be regretted.

Oundle, Mill Road c1950 O103027

West of the town centre, Mill Street climbs uphill to West Street and remains little altered since the 1950s, although the bus stop has gone. On the left are the paired chimneys of the 1877 courthouse, now no longer a magistrate's court and partly occupied by the Oundle Museum. The church with its octagonal central tower was built in the 1870s and is now the Roman Catholic Church of the Holy Name of Jesus.

◀ **Oundle**
School Science Block c1950
O103018
With Laxton's motto 'God Grant Grace' below his heraldic shield adorning the buildings, the school expanded and since the 1950s has taken over a number of the older buildings in the centre of Oundle. This building, the School Science Block, however, is on the Glapthorn Road beyond New Street and dates from 1914. It is a distinguished Jacobean styled structure complete with an onion domed cupola.

Oundle, Laxton and Crosby School Houses c1950 O103010
Oundle School, now a leading public school, started out as a small 16th century grammar school. Founded (or refounded) by Sir William Laxton in 1556, a prosperous London grocer, it remained modest until the mid 19th century, when it grew rapidly. A large number of its fine stone buildings now dominate the north part of the town. They are mostly Victorian and earlier 20th century, and the majority are in the Jacobean or Gothic style as seen here - the favoured architectural styles of most Victorian public schools.

Stanion, The Village c1960
S627001
This view from the fields south-east of Stanion shows the small Northamptonshire village centred on the medieval church, with its fine 15th-century tower with broach spire. The electricity pylons march towards Corby just over the distant horizon. By 1960, the village was surrounded by housing estates. The woods conceal former ironstone quarries that fed the iron making industry of Corby.

Stanion, Shop and Cardigan Arms, Cardigan Road c1965 S627007
Now within the village, Frith's photographer looks down one of the estate roads, with their undistinguished 'Anywheresville' modern houses, towards the High Street. The Cardigan Arms is on the left, its single storey flat-roofed outbuilding straight ahead. The shop has closed and been converted to a chalet bungalow while the thatched cottage in the distance has lost its thatch.

Corby, Stewart and Lloyd's Steel Works c1955 C337005
Long a centre of iron and steel making, using the iron-rich local limestone, Corby already had a vast 1930s steelworks and a population of about 15,000 swamping the original small village when it was designated a New Town in 1950 under the New Towns Act of 1946. This view shows the Stewart and Lloyds Steel Works with its numerous railway sidings. Later to become part of British Steel, it is now part of the privatised Corus.

▼ **Corby, High Street c1955** C337012

The High Street of the old village, now traffic calmed, has shops somewhat marred by security shutters, but in the 1950s all that was in the future. It is a curious contrast of building styles, ranging from the fine thatched stone house dated 1609 in the distance to the mundane brick of John Manners Ltd, now an engineering supplies store. The trees and gate piers on the right have been replaced by a 1960s close of old people's bungalows, named St Andrew's Walk. The modern town centre is well to the west around Corporation Street and the Market Square.

▼ **Corby, Rockingham Road c1955** C337019

This long terrace of shops with flats above is typical of the earlier growth of Corby. The further terrace is unchanged but the nearer one, on the corner of Telfords Lane, has had its leaking roofs renewed and the parapet removed. The central raised section of the parapet is now incorporated in a gable. The shops have undergone many changes since this view was taken.

▲ **Corby, Odeon Cinema c1955** C337001

The Odeon Cinema is built in a contrasting architectural style - a sort of Art Deco with rendered walls and rusticated ground floor a befits a venue to escape from the everyday. Here the Odeon is showing 'Silver City' starring Randolph Scott and Barbara Britton. Sadly, the Odeon is now no longer a cinema but a furniture warehouse and the ground floor has been much altered.

◄ **Corby, The Phoenix, Beanfield Avenue c1965** C337103
The Phoenix and the attached shopping precinct to the west of the modern town centre are typical examples of the late 1950s to early 1960s New Town expansion. Much of it is flat roofed and the pub is virtually unchanged, except for the name sign. Its frontage facing the road is severe and almost without windows, only the landlord's flat above, with its characteristic 1960s zig-zag tiles, has sizeable windows. The section to the left is the first shop in the precinct with its central car park.

Rockingham, The Castle c1960 R353009

By complete contrast, our tour now enters feudal Northamptonshire with this fine castle. Although relatively little of the medieval castle remains, the highlight is undoubtedly the late 13th-century gatehouse with the arched gateway flanked by massive drum towers. Described as ruinous in the earlier 16th century, the castle's character beyond the mighty walls is now that of a Tudor and 17th-century country house. The Watson family have lived here since 1553 and it is sometimes open it to the public.

Rockingham, Post Office c1955 R353018

The pretty ironstone village, once a market town, descends the lower slopes of the ridge along the Uppingham Road. It is a delightful village with mostly 18th-century houses, with a sprinkling of 19th-century estate cottages, such as those with the slate-roofed dormers on the left, dated 1858. The shop is now gone but the telephone kiosk remains. The taller building with dormers, in the middle distance, is the Sondes Arms, a coaching inn in the 18th century.

Around Kettering and Rothwell

Kettering, Sheep Street c1955 K13045
In the 1950s Kettering was still an important boot and shoe town, specialising in heavy work boots. It also had a significant engineering and clothing industry. The views here concentrate on the historic core of the market town. In this view are three of the best buildings in the town: the medieval parish church; the more modern columned art gallery of 1913, which was built to house the work of a noted local artist, Alfred East; and next to that, by the bus, the fine library of 1904. Piccadilly Buildings on the left date from 1926. Little is changed in this view now, apart from the more stylish modern bus shelters.

Kettering, Parish Church c1955 K13030
The approach to the church is from Sheep Street, along a gravelled tree-lined avenue through memorial gates. These were erected in memory of the Roughton family, who served the town as doctors continuously from 1738 until 1933. The avenue leads to the superb west tower of Saints Peter and Paul church. Its grandeur recalls the pre-boot and shoe era of the sheep trade, from which the town gained its earlier wealth.

Kettering, High Street c1955 K13027

The architecture of the High Street reflects the wealth that a depressed town gained from its booming boot and shoe industry in later Victorian times. The Royal Hotel on the left was built in 1878, while the banks are among the grandest buildings of that confident era. These survive today. Many of the buildings in the middle distance, however, were swept away in the decades after the 1950s. The 1930s modernistic Granada cinema remains, although it is now Gala Bingo.

Kettering, Silver Street c1955 K13022

East of the High Street and parallel to it, Silver Street leads us out of the market place. On the left next to 'Phipps' is 'The Rising Sun', a Jacobean styled extravaganza of 1892. Today it's a garishly painted theme bar, the 'Bar Sun'. On the right is Burtons, built in 1932 in the company's usual Art Deco Classical style. Today it is an estate agents.

Kettering, The Bridge, Wicksteed Park c1955 K13003

South-east of the town, along the valley of the River Ise and west of Barton Seagrave village, is The Wicksteed Park with the river dammed to form a large lake as the centrepiece. Around it is a large amusement park, started in the 1930s and still going strong today. The many entertainments include a fairground, boating lake and aviaries. This view shows the boat station by the 1936 hump-backed bridge. Nowadays there is also an elevated monorail. All the buildings, including the distant flat-roofed chalets, survive today.

Kettering, Miniature Railway, Wicksteed Park c1955 K13012

Circling the lake, which is nearly a third of a mile long and 200 yards wide in places, is a miniature railway. It deviates briefly into the parkland, as shown in this view. In the 1950s the carriages were open flat-bed trucks with what look remarkably like park benches to sit on. Nowadays the seating is very different and the coaches have roofs above their open sides, but otherwise this rather unfashionable railway and park are still thriving and immensely popular with the people of Kettering.

Barton Seagrave, Old Cottages c1955 B7000
Immediately east of Wicksteed Park, on the higher ground above the River Ise, Barton Seagrave has a small co of stone-built houses and cottages and a goo Norman church around a triangular green. To th south are large modern housing estates. This view looks north toward Barton Seagrave Hall, just visible beyond the tall lime trees. Since the 1950s, the cottages hav been restored and a roa now cuts close to them.

◀ **Barton Seagrave, Barton Seagrave Hall c1960**
B700014
This is a fine house, dated 1725, but with an older inner core. Now a home for the elderly, its main frontage has gabled end wings and a central porch. This view looks east to the side of the west wing, which is big enough to be a house in its own right.

Isham, South Street c1955 131037

South of Kettering, the village of Isham's best parts lie east of the main Wellingborough Road. Here we look along Middle Street with Little Thatches on the left, its windows now painted white. The thatched cottages beyond have been all but demolished, but the front walls remain as part of a flat roofed house called The Old Workshop.

Isham, Kettering Road c1950 131035

This view has changed a lot since 1950 due to the increase in traffic. The Old Red Lion on the right survives but is renamed The Monk and Minstrel. In the foreground there is now a bus shelter erected in 1953, Coronation Year. Beyond, the trees and walls have made way for a wider road. Most of the buildings on the left survive, with the pantiled building behind the white cottage much altered and now the village shop, 'Ram News'.

Geddington, The Church c1955 G84009

Geddington, by-passed by the A43, is a delightful stone-cottaged backwater. Here the photographer looks south-east towards the church of St Mary Magdalene. The village shop, with its prominent Woodbine and Capstan cigarette advertisements, has since been converted into a house. The church has an Anglo-Saxon nave and much 13th-century work, as well as a 14th-century clerestory and chancel.

◄ **Geddington, The Square c1955** G84013

Apart from the signs and the Pre-War Morris car, little has changed here. The Star Inn still looks out towards the wonderful, elegant stone cross on its seven step base. The tall cross, with its statues in their canopied niches, is the best surviving Eleanor Cross - one of a series erected by the distraught King Edward I wherever his wife Eleanor of Castile's coffin rested overnight on its journey from Nottinghamshire to London in 1290. The other cross in Northamptonshire, at Hardingstone, also survives.

Geddington, The Ford c1955 G84029
This view looks across the River Ise towards the parish church with its graceful 15th-century tower and tall
recessed spire. To its left is an 18th-century house with a sundial dated 1767 in the central dormer window. The
ford is still in use, as is the narrow, much repaired and altered 13th-century stone bridge.

Desborough, High Street c1960 D200009
Desborough, a small stone-built town, on the A6 to Leicester (turnpiked in the 1720s), once had many hand-loom weavers and woolcombers until the demise of this home-based industry at the end of the 18th century. In the 1820s silk-weaving became the main business to some extent, until later in the century when boot, shoe and clothing factories arrived.

Desborough, Corset Factory c1960 D200023a
This large, late 19th-century factory is still in production with brands including Rigby and Peller of London. It supplies corsets to the nobility and gentry, as well as swimwear and underwear for lesser mortals, all under the umbrella of Eveden Ltd. The road in this view is now a lay-by on the A6.

**Desborough
Station Road c1965**
D200038
This view of Station
Road looks south-
west past the junction
to Havelock Street,
with the imposing
clock tower of the
1903 Co-op store.
Havelock Street is a
terrace of Victorian
artisan cottages, while
Station Road remains
the principal shopping
street. The Co-op is still
the Co-op but with a
less attractive modern
shopfront.

Desborough, Rushton Road c1955 D200019
Rushton Road, at the east end of Station Road, is a mix of Victorian terrace housing and factories. Cheaney's, on the right, is a 1930s rebuild of a shoe manufacturer established in 1886 and still in business today. Desborough's character as a workaday town is illustrated rather well here.

Rushton Hall, The Lodge Gates c1955 R272005
From industrial Desborough we move three miles east to the quiet village of Rushton. West of the village are the grounds of Rushton Hall where Sir Thomas Tresham, the zealous Roman Catholic convert, once lived around 1600. This view is of the east lodges - early 19th-century confections of 'Gothick' built for the Cokaynes and now the entrance to Rushton Hall School for blind and visually handicapped children.

Rushton, Triangular Lodge 1952 R272011
This remarkable triangular building was erected for the Roman Catholic enthusiast Sir Thomas Tresham in the 1590s as a physical manifestation of the Holy Trinity. Full of triangles, multiples of three and the Tresham trefoil badge, it is now an English Heritage site, open to the public and well worth a visit.

Rushton, The Parish Church c1955 R272003
The village lies east of Rushton Hall's park. This view looks east, the road curving past the churchyard towards the hipped roofed Thornhill Arms in the distance. The 14th-century church is mostly in ironstone with paler Weldon limestone battlements in the tower.

Rushton, Manor Road c1955 R272001
Manor Road joins the High Street by the pyramid roofed mid-19th century house, The Forge, in the distance. To the right, is a small wing with the date 1852 over a Gothic-style stone window. Built as a schoolroom, it is now part of the house. Opposite are semi-detached early 1950s rural district council houses.

Rothwell, Church Walk c1955 R322009
Rothwell is an old town with a market charter from King John's reign. Built around its fine market place, it found new life in the 19th century when it joined Northamptonshire boot and shoe industry with several factories and terraces of hard red Midland brick houses. This view looks east from the High Street to the west tower of the large medieval parish church. To the left is a former manor house, once the Urban District Council offices.

◀ **Rothwell, High Street c1955** R322026
Here the photographer looks north along the High Street, towards its junction with Bridge Street to the right, and Desborough Road curving left. The proudly pedimented Midland Bank is now Peter M Ayres clothes shop while R Walker on the left has become Alistair Mackay's antiques and clocks. The Crown Hotel is unchanged and still retains its attractive and unusual hanging sign.

Rothwell, The Charnel House c1955 R322015
Frith's photographer takes us down into the crypt of Holy Trinity church, discovered by an 18th-century gravedigger when the aisle floor collapsed beneath him. In it he found a vaulted 13th-century ossuary, or charnel house, containing the bones from over 1500 human skeletons from the graveyard. They remain there, neatly stacked.

▼ Rothwell, Jesus Hospital c1955 R322006
South of the church, and facing the market place, is Jesus Hospital which was founded in 1591 for 26 poor men. It surrounds a quadrangle, the roof of the oldest part, dated 1593, is just visible to the left. This view shows the entrance range of 1840, with the finialled original 1590s gateway (behind a Pre-War Austin 10). They are still almshouses, although now converted to flats where the occupants live rent-free.

► Rothwell Market House c1965
R322053
The Market House was built for Sir Thomas Tresham of Rushton Hall. Originally with its ground floor open behind the arches, it was left unfinished, amazingly, for over three centuries, and finally completed in 1895. It is a curious Tudor 'alien' in the Georgian and Victorian town centre. The building behind was demolished in 1965, but that on the left, dated 1710, survives.

▲ **Rothwell
Market Place c1955**
R322023
This view looks east from
Bridge Street, past the
Market House and along
into Bell Hill. On the right
is the former Coffee Tavern
in a building dated 1710,
and beyond that the side
roof of The Woolpack,
its building dated 1714.
Beyond the approaching
car, is part of the tall gable
wall of the Stanley Works,
which was still functioning
as a boot and shoe factory
in the1950s.

Wellingborough and the Industrial Nene Valley

Wellingborough, River Nene and Victoria Mills c1965 W279054
Whitworth Brothers Flour Mills stand beside the A509 London Road bridge. These vast buildings, the brick ones in part dated 1886, are well known landmarks when approaching Wellingborough from the south. The river bridge has now been rebuilt and widened, while the house and warehouse (right) have gone to make way for the by-pass.

Wellingborough, Sheep Street c1955 W279032a
This view looks south, downhill past Horden's booksellers and stationers, which is undergoing repair. The scaffolding, with the workman standing casually, thumbs in waistcoat pocket, belongs to a different era as far as safety concerns go. The shopfront survives, now as an opticians but Wright and Sons next door is now a two storey flat roofed building.

Wellingborough, Swanspool House c1955 W279037
This rendered three storey house with its central Venetian windows above the doorway was the headquarters of Wellingborough Urban District Council. Since local government re-organisation in 1974, it has belonged to Wellingborough Borough Council

Wellingborough, The Hind Hotel c1955 W279009
At the top of Sheep Street is the largely 17th-century Hind Hotel, perhaps the best secular building in the town. It serves as a reminder of the distinction of this stone town before it was transformed by industrialisation in the 19th century. Oliver's cocktail bar and coffee lounge is now next door (left).

◄ **Wellingborough**
Market Street c1955 W279029
This view looks south along Market Street past the Midland Road junction towards Sheep Street. Most buildings in the foreground survive, albeit with their shopfronts altered and with different tenants. The tall domed building on the left survives as a Burton's clothes store, but the building beyond, with the conical roofed turret, was demolished as part of the 1990s Swansgate shopping centre redevelopment.

Wellingborough, Midland Street c1955 W279046
From the Hind Hotel we walk down Market Street and turn right down Midland Road. All the buildings on the left have been replaced by the modern Swansgate shopping centre. Other change includes the demolition of the stuccoed Midland Hotel on the right. The Old King's Arms at the end of the road is now a carpet store.

Wellingborough Zoo Park c1950 W279017
Off the west side of Sheep Street, a plaque informs us that the Zoo Park was opened in the grounds of the historic Croyland Abbey in 1943. Once home to large animals like this tiger, in the middle enclosure, the site is now occupied by offices.

Wellingborough, Wilby Swimming Pool c1960
W279013
The 1950s was the last decade of the supremacy of the open air pool. Most were rebuilt or covered over and replaced by the modern heated indoor pool. Here we see one on the outskirts of the town, now supplanted by the covered and heated 1960s Wellingborough Swimming Pool off Croyland Road.

Wellingborough School c1955 W279040
Here we see an independent co-educational day school for children aged from three to 18 years. This view looks at the first school buildings on the site, built from 1879 to 1895. Many others followed in the 1960s and 70s, and the school occupies most of the south side of the road, with its playing fields extending close to the River Nene.

Finedon, Church Hill c1955 F184007
Finedon has had a market charter since at least 1294 and the older part of the town, pictured here, lies at the west end. It became yet another of Northamptonshire's boot and shoe manufacturing towns in the later 19th century and was greatly enlarged, with streets of Victorian terrace housing. This view includes the medieval chancel of the superb parish church, seen looming over the left hand cottage.

Finedon, The Bell Inn (Oldest in England) c1955 F184004
The older part of the village is full of houses and cottages built by the Victorian lord of the manor, William Mackworth-Dolben. None are more fanciful than The Bell Inn on Bell Hill. It was rebuilt, transforming an earlier, possibly 17th-century building, in 1872 - and apparently originates from 1042 as the Tingdene Hostelrie, a monastic hospice for travellers.

Finedon, Independent Wesleyan Chapel c1955 F184011
In the centre of the village, on Affleck Bridge, is the Independent Wesleyan Chapel built in 1874 to serve the Nonconformist industrial workers of the boot and shoe factories. Beyond it, the shop has since been demolished and replaced by a 1970s flat-roofed health centre. 1950s council houses in Dolben Square are visible on the left.

▼ **Finedon, The War Memorial, c1955** F184015
Wellingborough Road is home to the War Memorial in its railing enclosure.
Each side bears a single uplifting word to describe the attributes of the soldiers
of Finedon who died in World War I – 'prowess', 'cheerfulness', 'courage' and
'endurance'.

▼ **Irthlingborough, High Street 1969** I33020
This is not one of Northamptonshire's most attractive boot and shoe towns - and
what old buildings remain are now isolated by new buildings, some visible in
this view. The house on the right was rebuilt in the 1970s and others have been
rendered, with few original windows surviving. The Victorian chapel on the right
is now an auction saleroom.

▲ **Irthlingborough
The Cross 1969** I33023
This view, looking into
the High Street from
the market square, is
distinguished by the
crocketted and slender
medieval Market
Cross - a reminder of
Irthlingborough's 11th-
century market town
origins. The National
Provincial Bank on the
right is now the post
office, while the shops on
the left have since been
demolished to make way
for a car park.

◀ **Irthlingborough
Bull Hotel and Cross
c1955** I33314
Another view of the Market
Cross, this time looking
north, shows its knobbly
crockets to their best
advantage. The cross at
the top of the shaft was
lost many years before.
The Bull Hotel, rebuilt in
the 1930s, is a somewhat
pedestrian and incongruous
mock-Tudor effort, while
the house on the left is now
a bistro.

Islip, Church and Lychgate c1955 I56002
Continuing along the west side of the River Nene as it heads north-east, we reach Islip. The river forms the parish boundary with Thrapston, now a small industrial town on the east bank. Islip remains a small village, with mostly stone cottages and houses. This view looks through the 1903 lychgate towards the crocketted spire of the 15th-century parish church.

Islip House, Country Club c1960 156009

From the Thrapston bank of the River Nene, the photographer looks across to the former Country Club. A fine Georgian house, it boasts a Colleyweston slate roof and sash windows. The creeper has gone and the render has now been colourwashed. The rear elevation, and what used to be service buildings, are made of stone.

Islip, The Bridge c1960 156003

This view of the bridge was taken from near Islip House, on the west bank. In 1795, the medieval bridge was seriously damaged by floods and five of its nine arches were washed away. Although they were later rebuilt, little of the original structure remains. There is now an additional concrete footbridge along this side, the main part being reserved for motor vehicles.

◄ **Thrapston**
Midland Road c1955
T104009
Thrapston is a small medieval market town engulfed in 19th- and 20th-century housing and factories. The views in this book concentrate on this mostly red brick and slate element of the town's architectural history. This view looks north along Midland Road, its name deriving from the old railway station. The terraces and villas shown are all intact today.

Thrapston
The Nine Arches Bridge
c1955 T104010
This view is also from the Islip bank, but further upstream. The houses in the distance have been demolished. The reed beds along the river were once harvested for the local Loveday family, who produced baskets, horse collars, chair seats and other products. Their workshops closed in 1960.

Thrapston
De Vere Road c1955
T104013
By way of contrast, Frith's photographer looks along De Vere Road. Pairs of 1930s semis seem to march down the hill, the view made more bleak by the brutal municipal pruning of the silver birch trees - they are now no more substantial than the street lamp or the telephone line pole.

Thrapston
Oundle Road c1960
T104035
Here we see more late Victorian and Edwardian terraces and villas, mostly built of brick or roughcast. The road curves towards the town centre, passing the end of De Vere Road. The shop in the distance is now a bigger 'One-Stop Shop'. At the far end are the two gabled bays of the Old Rectory.

▼ Thrapston, The Lakes c1960 T104031

All along the Nene valley hereabouts are flooded iron ore pits, some of which have been turned into fishing or boating lakes. There is more development here now, with a yacht club boathouse and more leisure facilities to suit modern expectations.

▼ Raunds, Market Square c1955 R82016

Moving south from Thrapston we reach Raunds, another small Northamptonshire market town transformed into a Victorian boot and shoe manufacturing town. The best feature of the town is undoubtedly the parish church with its lofty 13th-century tower. To the right is the George and Dragon pub.

**▲ Raunds
Brook Street c1955**

R82025

Further south, the High Street becomes Brook Street as it heads toward the unromantically named Hog Dyke. To the right are the walls and gate piers of the Methodist Church built in 1874. The post office next door is now clad in painted roughcast and the buildings beyond that have been demolished.

◄ **Stanwick**
The Duke of Wellington
c1965 S628003
Stanwick is a village two miles south-west of Raunds. In 1960 Phipps was taken over by the giant Watney-Mann brewery, which retained the Phipps name but introduced the lettering shown here. Particularly poignant is the barrel over the inn sign, a reminder of Watneys Red Barrel - a truly awful keg beer that almost singlehandedly led to the Campaign for Real Ale.

Higham Ferrers, Market Square c1955 H245022
Higham Ferrers is undoubtedly the smartest town, architecturally, in the boot and shoe belt that runs east along the River Nene from Wollaston to Thrapston. It is most famous for the superb church and the 15th-century Archbishop Chichele Bede House and School. Note the quality of its stone houses, albeit with some later brickwork. The chemist's shop is still a chemist's.

Higham Ferrers, Market Square c1955 H245007
This view shows the market cross on the left, a cone of stone replacing the original stepped base. Beyond it stands the 1809 town hall. On the right is a fine Georgian house, once a shop owned by Horsley Ltd. Today the premises sells motorcycles.

Rushden, The War Memorial c1965 R223018
Rushden, which merges to the north with Higham Ferrers, does not have a great deal of interest architecturally – except for its superb parish church, with a tower and spire nearly 164 ft high. The war memorial is of an unusual octagonal design and beyond is the, now traffic-choked, High Street.

Rushden, High Street c1960 R223031
Mostly the buildings are two storey. Banks, such as Lloyds in this view, are the only buildings of any quality. It is a workaday street - the white railway bridge in the distance has now gone, along with the railway track. The line, which opened in 1893, ran from Higham Ferrers to Wellingborough Midland Road, and closed to passenger services in 1959 and to freight in 1969.

Irchester, Knuston Hall Education Centre c1960 I71028a
Between Rushden and Urchester lies Knuston Hall, situated in parkland leading down to an artificial lake.
A complex house architecturally with 17th-, 18th- and 19th-century elements, it has long been owned by
Northamptonshire County Council and used for residential and day courses. Now 'Knuston Hall Conference
Centre and College of Adult Education,' it is well known for its thatching courses.

Irchester, High Street c1955 I71007
The village expanded with the boot and shoe works in the later 19th century, but the original stone village survives. Irchester, as the name suggests, was a Roman town and some earthworks survive nearer the River Nene. These stone cottages were demolished in the 1950s and the site is now the access road to St Katherine's Way. Behind is the spire of the medieval parish church.

Irchester, High Street c1955 I71005
The High Street continues north, downhill towards the parish church, while the through road was widened and improved in 1950s. The result was the removal of the bay windowed 1890s houses on the far right. Otherwise little has changed.

Irchester, The War Memorial c1960 I71025a
Here we can see the war memorial at the junction of High Street, Wollaston Road and Farndish Road, with steps leading up to the tall monument surmounted by a cross. There is an additional poignant plaque at its foot commemorating an air raid on 20th May 1941, in which nine villagers were killed. Beyond are 1890s houses, now unpleasantly re-windowed.

Wollaston, Hickmire c1955 W421003
Wollaston is a small market town with a charter granted in 1260 and with the remains of a motte and bailey castle. It slumbered until Victorian times when the boot and shoe industry and the manufacture of rush matting arrived. Expansion continued into in the 20th century. The best of the old village is around the parish church, particularly in the quaintly named street, Hickmire.

Wollaston, The Square c1955 W421009
The architectural quality falls off somewhat in the southern part of the town. This view looks along the London Road to The Square, with Hinwick Road to the left. The Nags Head dominates with its 1880s gabled bay and oriel windows. The clock was installed in 1953 to commemorate the coronation of Queen Elizabeth II. The Shell garage on the right has been rebuilt, now for UK Petroleum.

◄ **Wollaston
Park Street c1955**
W421015
Wollaston expanded farther
after World War II and this
view is of former council
housing, part of an estate
built in the south-east of the
town. Looking south past
the junction with Queens
Road, the houses are little
changed, apart from being
fitted with ubiquitous
plastic windows (apart
from No 10 on the corner).
The elegant swan's neck
concrete lampposts have
mostly been replaced by
galvanised metal ones.

◀ **Wollaston**
High Street c1955 W421014
The High Street runs northwards, parallel to the through road to Irchester. It is a narrow road with a mix of architectural styles and has suffered much rebuilding since the 1950s. A 1970s terrace replaces the pebble-dashed terrace on the right. The Boot Inn, an 18th-century painted stone and thatched-roofed building, survives, while the shop beyond is now Whibley's, a newsagent and general store.

▼ **Bozeat, The Chequers c1955** B701005
Bozeat, now by-passed by the A609, has since regained some of its tranquillity. Boot and shoe manufacturing led to the expansion of the village in the late 19th century, as it did in many Northamptonshire villages in this area. This view on the London Road reflects the changes brought about by the by-pass. The Chequers ceased to be a pub, although traces of the painted signs on the front wall can still be seen. The thatched cottage next to it has gone also, although bits have been retained as a garden wall.

◀ **Bozeat**
High Street c1955 B701012
Road improvements in the 1960s swept away these stone houses to make way for the greater convenience of the motorist. The mature cyclist is about to free-wheel into the High Street off to the right. Note the Brooke Bond Tea advertisement – its packets included picture cards, collected eagerly by myself and numerous other children in the 1950s. Bozeat concludes our tour of industrial Northamptonshire.

Northampton and Central Northamptonshire

Northampton
Market Place c1950 N40009
This chapter starts in the county town of
Northampton – in its superb and large market
square. Looking north, every building in this view
has been demolished, including the grandiose
Emporium Arcade of 1901 and the modernistic
Mercury and Herald offices to its right. Together
with an entire street, Newland (right), all were
replaced by the 1970s Grosvenor Centre
shopping malls. The elaborate fountain, erected to
commemorate the wedding of Prince Edward, later
Edward VII, and Princess Alexandra in 1863 was
demolished in 1962.

**Northampton
Market Place c1950**
N40011
A market place since at least 1235, the west side shown here survives much better than the north side. On close examination today, 'Kendalls' (left of centre) was rebuilt in the 1970s as a vague facsimile, and 'Man's Shop' was redesigned in aggressive 1960s glass and concrete frame style. On market days today, the market place is packed with stalls with cheerful green and white striped awnings, and there is no car park.

▼ **Northampton, Mercers Row c1955** N40025

Mercers Row leads west from the market place, with the parish church of All Saints to its left. It was largely rebuilt after a disastrous fire in 1675 which destroyed most of the town centre. On the right is 'Timothy White and Taylor', a 1950s chemists chain, once the main rival of Boots, itself seen in the distance. Boots has now moved into the Grosvenor Centre, while Timothy White and Taylor did not survive the 60s.

▼ **Northampton, Gold Street c1955** N40057

At the junction of Gold Street and Bridge Street, with The Drapery to the right, this view looks west from the end of Mercers Row. Note the splendid 1930s period lettering of 'T C Palmer', the clothes shop, advertising its hand tailored clothes. Most buildings here survive, although further down Gold Street, around the Horse Fair, there have been dramatic changes.

▲ **Northampton, Abingto Street c1955** N40002

Abington Street, now partly pedestrianised, sa considerable changes after this view was taken. Most evocative of past shopping is The Fifty Shilling Tailors, a chain that grew up before World War II and originally offered suits fo that price. It occupied a building dated 1677, one of the first rebuilt after the 1675 fire. The building survives, but Th Fifty Shilling Tailor is no more. Its rival opposite, in the 1930s Burton building, still survives.

Northampton, Abington Street c1955 N40051
Further along Abington Street at the much rebuilt east end, the austere building with the pyramid roofs was once the Notre Dame High School, built in 1871. A school and convent run by the Sisters of Notre Dame de Namur, it was demolished in 1975 and replaced by a higher yielding commercial concern. On the left is the New Theatre, regrettably demolished in 1960 – its passing bemoaned as a consequence of television (which also closed six cinemas in the town.)

**Duston
Main Road c1960**
D202026
After a long but
ultimately fruitless
resistance, Duston
was absorbed into
Northampton's borough
boundary in 1965. This
view shows the slightly
disjointed mix of
17th- and 18th-century
stone cottages (many
thatched), a few larger
farmhouses and houses,
some Victorian cottages
(one pair dated 1875),
and one or two more
modern ones. The
single decker bus
is heading to
Northampton.

◄ **Duston**
Main Road c1955 D20201C
Looking beyond the
Squirrels Inn sign, the
pedimented Congregational
Chapel on the right was
demolished in the 1960s
and replaced by a modern
up-to-the-minute chapel
with an attached hall by A
W Walker. The baker's with
its characteristic 'Hovis' sign
is still a baker's, and Duston
retains other shops, unlike
many Northamptonshire
villages.

◀ Duston, Squirrels Inn c1955

D202012

The Squirrels Inn, on the corner of Squirrel Lane, is virtually unchanged - an attractive ironstone building with a thatched roof. In 1955 a Phipps and Company tied house, the brewery merged shortly afterwards with the Northampton Brewery Company to become Phipps Northampton Brewery Company. It was taken over by Watney-Mann in 1960 in part of the then massive nationwide shake-up of the brewing industry. In front is a weird Morris Eight, with timber framed shooting brake character, a veteran of the 1930s.

▼ Duston, British Timken c1955

D202020

Just east of the village, where Main Road curves towards Bants Lane, is this large factory which employed over 3,000 people in the 1960s. Two storey offices screen the vast factory behind, where bearings and specialist steel castings and fabrications are made. Now just known as Timken, these elegant offices remain as a tribute to the architectural quality and care given to such buildings, even in wartime. It was opened in 1942.

◀ Moulton
Cross Street c1955 M295003

Moulton is a village of narrow winding lanes, lined by stone-built cottages and houses, nowadays with traffic calming and one-way systems. The stone-built Gothicky Methodist Chapel of 1835 with its pretty arched windows is next to the old school of 1878, now used by the Moulton Theatre. Unfortunately the tranquillity of this view is somewhat spoilt today by the level of traffic, mostly cars, snaking through the village's narrow lanes.

▼ Moulton, Implement Gates c1955 M295004

These gates, with agricultural implements incorporated, are situated at the Holly Lodge on the Boughton Road west of the village. They are apposite, for Moulton College of Agriculture occupies the land north of Moulton village. Now known as Moulton College and the Hulcot Centre, it still serves the same function, with the addition of a farm produce shop. Most of the agricultural college buildings date from the 1930s.

▼ Overstone, Lake Side c1955 O104052

Overstone Park has for years been a leisure facility for nearby Northampton. Nowadays it combines a golf, hotel and leisure resort with residential lodges and a caravan park, all located around sizeable lakes. The Victorian Gothic pile of a country house is now Overstone Park School, situated in the centre of the vast park. This view was taken by the eastern lake.

▲ Overstone, The Solarium Hotel c1955 O104020

At the eastern edge, Overstone Manor, an elegant classical style 1930s building, is now a pub, restaurant and hotel. The park was and is a popular location for caravan and other rallies – it hosted the 1963 National Caravan Rally. This view shows an earlier rally with an orderly queue for drinks. The bottles look like milk bottles. Note how caravans have progressed since the 1950s plywood era.

◄ **Overstone, The Swimming Pool c1955**

O104040

The next two views were taken around the swimming pool north of Overstone Manor. They are typical scenes from the more hardy 1950s, when the country was dotted with open air pools and lidos. The changing room and seating shelter is built in classical style, while Tudor fake timber-framing, complete with a thatched roof, is the style of the main building.

**Overstone
The Swimming Pool
c1955** O104039
Behind the thatched
building are some of
the fine trees of the
park. The north-east
quarter of Overstone
Park is heavily
wooded. Along the
Sywell Road, from
the 1950s on, closes
of expensive houses
were built within
the park boundary,
retaining many of the
specimen trees. There
was once an old village
of Overstone near to
the grandiose main
mansion, but this was
moved in 1821 and
estate cottages built
along the boundary.

◄ **Earls Barton
The Village c1955** E97005
This view is taken further
down West Street, with the
churchyard on the left and
the boundary walls of the
Victorian Baptist Church
on the right. The church
dominates views from the
south while behind it, to
the north, are the remains
of the Norman motte and
bailey castle. Remarkably,
the brutally pruned lime
trees survive. Note the
1950s swan's neck concrete
street lamp, now replaced.

Earls Barton, West Street
c1965 E97021
Our brief foray into parkland is over and we reach Earls Barton, some six miles east of Northampton. Called Earls Barton because of its connections with the earls of Northampton, it is mainly noted for its powerful Anglo-Saxon church tower, seen here dominating the view. The village is an architectural mix with older stone houses set amid Victorian brick and slate, and modern 20th-century homes.

Earls Barton
The Square c1965 E97027
At the junction with Station Road, Frith's photographer stands by the war memorial with the churchyard behind him. The tall building behind Underwood's shop (now The Corner Shop) is the old Harcourt shoe factory - recently converted into flats and a sound studio. The Earls Barton Museum is hidden by the trees on the right. The museum is housed in what was once Barker's shoe factory.

Castle Ashby, The House c1955
C224014
We now move away from boot and shoe country into the south of Northamptonshire close to the border with Buckinghamshire. Here, at the centre of what is still one of Northamptonshire's largest estates, a vast Elizabethan mansion replaces a ruined castle. Its construction was started in 1574 by the Comptons, who later became earls of Northampton, and the great courtyard house was completed in the earlier 17th century. It is famous for its unusual 1624 balustrade with, instead of balusters, letters forming a quotation from Psalm 127.

Castle Ashby, The Church c1955 C224006
The mansion and the church sit amid a park of over 200 acres, in an estate of more than 10,000 acres. The church is to the east of the house and looks like a personal chapel, as the village is further away to the west beyond the gates. The church appears to be an appendage to the house and its balustrades include inscriptions written in English. The one here is taken from Jesus' saying about the lilies of the field: 'Solomon in all his glory was not arrayed like one of them'.

Yardley Hastings, The Square c1955 Y43004
This view looks from Little Street into the somewhat grandly named The Square, where now the central tree is a forlorn stump. The house beyond, now enlarged, is the National Youth Resources Centre for the United Reformed Church. Young people can stay here either in single rooms or small dormitories. Next to it is the United Reformed Church, rebuilt in 1813 to replace an earlier church that was destroyed by fire.

Yardley Hastings, Little Lane c1952 Y43009
Note the topiary which still survives, although now less mathematically crisp-edged. The 18th-century thatched cottage on the left is joined now by more thatched roofs on the cottages beyond the topiary. In the foreground is one of the 1940s and 1950s most popular Triumph motor cycles: The Tiger twin cylinder.

Yardley Gobion, Village Green c1965 Y42009
Further west, on the Stony Stratford to Northampton road, is another Yardley. Now quieter, thanks to a bypass, it once had a wharf on the Grand Junction Canal which passed a quarter of a mile north of the village. This view gives a good idea of the village's architectural mix, with older stone cottages with thatched roofs, mid 19th-century cottages with sash windows and slate roofs, and to the left of the shop (now a house) the gables of 1960s brick estate-style houses.

Yardley Gobion, Moorend Road c1965 Y42012
The village expanded after World War II and this view along Moorend Road is an interesting example. Frith's photographer has focussed on the north side of the street with its interesting variety of stone cottages, while opposite, out of view, are modern 1960s houses which clearly did not grab his attention. The corrugated iron roofed house in the middle distance now has its thatch reinstated, while the shop in the distance is now a house.

Towcester, Watling Street c1955 T105007
In these last years before the M1 opened, Towcester was busy with traffic heading for Birmingham and the Midlands. Frith's photographer recorded it on a quiet day. Towcester has a long history, initially as a Roman fort and town called 'Lactodorum' located on the route the Anglo-Saxons called Watling Street which ran from Richborough in Kent to Shropshire. On the right is The Saracen's Head, a former coaching inn that features in Dickens' 'The Pickwick Papers'.

Towcester, Pickwick Restaurant c1960 T105036a
Watling Street has a good range of buildings, mostly dated 18th and 19th century, built in a mix of materials - stone, brick and render. The old Pickwick Restaurant recalls the Dickensian association with more dignity than its present name: 'The Pickled Pig'. Edwards' shop next door is now a dental care business, but the Pickwick's 18th-century shopfront survives.

Towcester
Town Hall c1965

T105027
Further south, Watling Street widens to form a market place complete with town hall and a corn exchange. The town received a market charter before 1220 and was an Anglo-Saxon fortified 'burh' since 917 AD. The town hall, built in Italianate style in 1865 with a central clocktower, is now divided into the offices belonging to the town council and other commercial concerns. To its left is the post office, located in an imposing brick fronted building of 1799. The market place still serves as a car park.

Towcester, The Brave Old Oak c1960 T105039

The Brave Old Oak pub with its fake timber-framing is a Phipps House here, and had just been taken over by brewers Watney Mann. Note the characteristic Watney's sloping lettering and the barrel over the inn sign - the symbol of the then voguish keg bitter that so nearly was to destroy real ale, in my opinion, in the 1960s. The chemist next door is now a bank. 'Phildelphus Jeyes' was a local business then, a branch of the chain set up by Philadelphus Jeyes of Northampton - the inventor of the disinfectant, Jeyes Fluid.

Towcester, River from the Bridge c1955 T105004

This view of the River Tove is taken from the bridge that crosses the river on the line the Romans set for Watling Street, where the road itself changes alignment from north-west to west-north-west. This view records the hay piled up to dry in the riverside meadow: - a sight that disappeared long ago to make way for a tyre company.

Towcester, Park Hall Gates c1955 T105019
South-east of the town on Watling Street, the entrance to Towcester Race Course and Conference Centre is through this fine gate screen linking two lodges. Built in 1822 it was originally an entrance to Easton Neston, Hawksmoor's great country house, set in a vast landscaped park north of the River Tove. The racecourse occupies the area south of the Tove and benefits greatly from such an elegant, albeit now secondary, entry.

**Blisworth
High Street c1965**
B283024
This village is less
well known than the
prodigious Grand
Junction Canal tunnel
that emerges just to
the south. The tunnel
is 3075 yards (2811
metres) long and was
a considerable feat
of engineering when
it opened in 1805.
The village is largely
stone built and was
surrounded by stone-
pits and small quarries
at one time. Later
brick houses also
feature, including the
Blisworth Post Office
and Stores in the
middle distance. The
corner shop advertising
Tizer is now a house.

Blisworth, The Elm Tree c1955 B283008
Only two of these cottages survived recent road
improvements. They include the one on the left
and the middle thatched dwelling on the right.
Ironically the new A43 Northampton road now by-
passes the village. The tree has also gone.

Milton Malsor, The Church c1955 M294003
Beyond Blisworth and virtually within earshot
of the M1 (which opened in the late 1950s)
Milton Malsor survives proximity to Northampton
remarkably well. A compact village with concentric
circles of winding, intimate lanes, the church has
a surprisingly timeless appearance with the field in
the foreground used for village fetes, including the
2002 Golden Jubilee fete. In this view the curious
stumpy 14th-century steeple sits atop a 13th-
century tower.

Milton Malsor, The War Memorial c1965 M294008
This view is in the heart of the village, where Green Street meets the High Street at a small green with a 1920s War Memorial cross. This is a scene of contrasts, featuring Manor Cottage, an 18th-century thatched stone-built house, and the dull 1960s house to the left. The bus shelter remains, but re-roofed in sheet metal.

Hardingstone, Primary School c1955 H418305
The photographer is looking west along the High Street, past the Victorian primary school with its cluster of steep slated pyramidal roofs and the hall 'erected by General Bouverie for the use of the parish 1866'. The foreground is now closed off by an extension of the stone wall and the railings.

Great Houghton
High Street c1965 G223008
This chapter ends at Great Houghton, south-east of Northampton.
It is a small village with a few modern closes. The White Hart pub
is little changed. Opposite is the gable of a 19th-century extension
to Stone House, a fine 17th-century house. Continuing south
there is a mix of older houses and 1960s dwellings, the shallow-
pitched gable of No 38 visible to the right of the electricity pole.

Daventry and West Northamptonshire

Daventry, The Moot Hall c1955 D83001

Daventry stagnated after the Railway Age as it was by-passed by the main line. Its profitable coach trade along Watling Street was also destroyed. These views capture the town just before the Daventry Development Corporation was formed in 1963. The population was to more than double and continues to grow apace. The decaying Moot Hall of 1769 dominates this view of the market square. It was later restored and now houses the Daventry Museum, the town mayor's parlour and the tourist information centre. Note the K2 telephone kiosk, a superb 1926 design by Sir Giles Gilbert Scott.

**Daventry
Market Square c1960**
D83025
This view looks across the market square towards Holy Cross Church, rebuilt in classical style in the 1750s with an unusual spire. The houses on the right survive, but those to the left of the monument were swept away and replaced by a small park, just one of many 'improvements' after 1963. The former National School of 1826 and 1870 is now an ex-servicemen's club. The impressive Gothic style memorial cross dates only from 1908 and, although as impressive as medieval Eleanor Cross, commemorates Edmund Charles Burton, a noted national hunt figure. It has now been relocated to the spot where the photographer stood.

**Daventry
High Street c1955**
D83009
Looking east along the High Street, this view gives a good idea of the variety of buildings and building materials to be found in this street, which survived modern development. As a consequence, it is something of an island amid a place of much change. It is now one way with very wide pavements. The cars add a nostalgic note with Morrises, Fords and Austins parked alongside the pavements.

▼ Daventry, Sheaf Street c1955 D83022

Sheaf Street did not survive modernisation and the buildings on the right, as far as the Dutch blind over the shop window, were swept away for the modern Foundry Walk shopping arcade. In the distance to the north, earlier housing estates, mostly Pre-War and 1950s, can be seen - the Development Corporation plans mainly expanded the town to the south and north-east.

▼ Daventry, Canal Tunnel c1955 D83014

A mile and a half north-east of Daventry, the Grand Junction (formerly the Grand Union) Canal cuts through the limestone ridge via the Braunston Tunnel. This view is of the east portal to the tunnel - it looks like any other canal bridge apart from the rusticated arch into the blackness. The house has been demolished, and to the left is the track for the barge horses who went overland to meet the barges at the other end of the tunnel.

▲ Braunston, High Street c1955 B778006

The Grand Union Canal emerges from the Braunston Tunnel east of Braunston village and descends past the village on a flight of six locks. This view looks west along the High Street. The pub on the right, a fine ironstone and thatch building, is now a house. The white-painted buildin was rebuilt in the 1960s a the village store and post office. On the far left is a rare sight amid the stone in this part of the county: a genuine timber-framed house, this one dated 14t century.

◀ **Braunston
The Canal c1965**
B778026
A little east of the
junction with the
Oxford Canal is the
bustling Braunston
Marina. Most of
the marina with its
boat-repairing shops,
boat hirers and the
chandlery remain today,
though the petrol tank
is now stored, wisely,
underground. Blocks
of 1980s flats and tall
riverside apartments
line the marina edge,
Brindley Quay.

Welton, The Cross Roads c1955 W477008
The parkland of 18th-century Welton Place sweeps south to the north bank of the Grand Union Canal, in its cutting leading to the east portal of the Braunston Tunnel. East of the park is the village, a figure of eight of winding lanes. This view looks east along Ashby Road to the small green at its junction with Station Road and High Street (to the right). The whitewashed cottage is Craven Cottage and is little changed today, but 1960s housing has appeared where the tall trees previously grew on the right.

Welton, The Village c1955 W477010a
Frith's photographer has moved into the High Street and is looking south towards The White Horse pub - which is little changed today. The outbuilding in front has been demolished for the enlargement of the pub car park. Beyond is the 14th-century tower of the parish church. The houses on the right side have not fared so well, either being altered or rebuilt, while the familiar 1930s designed telephone kiosk has been replaced by a modern one.

Lilbourne, Main Road c1955 L442005
The small village of Lilbourne had a market charter granted in 1219 by Henry III, but it clearly never developed into a fully fledged town. It also had a Norman motte and bailey castle whose earthworks survive quite well. This view, looking west from the green, has lost its two community facilities: The Bell is now a house, while the shop on the right is now a house called The Old Post Office.

Lilbourne, The Green c1955 L442006
The photographer here looks east towards Yelvertoft Road with Hillmorton Lane to the right. Just east of the village the peace is disrupted by Watling Street's successor, the busy M1 motorway. Major changes here since 1955 include modern 1960s houses, mostly bungalows, on Hillmorton Lane, beyond the signpost, and the telephone kiosk which has migrated to the foreground Green.

◄ **Welford**
West Street c1965
W577004

West Street is quieter than the High Street and this view looks south-west past the village hall with its somewhat ungainly porch 'perched' on the roof. The walls and buildings beyond belong to Welford Manor. Michael Ventris, the great archaeologist and decipherer of Minoan 'Linear B' script, is buried in the church yard at the end. He died in 1956 at a mere 34 years of age.

Welford, High Street c1965

W577015

The Leicester to Northampton road passes through Welford's High Street, parallel with the much more tranquil West Street. This view looks north-east and immediately you see the contrast with most other villages in this book - this is a mainly brick built village. We are now in the Lias clay country along the Leicestershire boundary. That said, the 18th-century Welford Manor, beyond the trees on the left, is built in stone.

Welford, The Canal c1965 W577012

The 'Welford Arm' runs east for one and a half miles from the Leicester branch of the Grand Union Canal and opened in 1814. Its main aim was to supply water to the main canal from Sulby Reservoir, and later Welford and Naseby reservoirs. This view is of the wharf at Welford. The canal fell into total disuse after World War II, but was restored and reopened in 1969.

Welford
Welford Reservoir
c1965 W577009

Welford Reservoir was constructed in 1837 to store and supply water to the Welford Arm which then fed the Leicester Arm of the Grand Union Canal. This view looks north along the grassy dam towards the bridge over the sluices. There is now a two ft high brick wall along the track.

◄ **Naseby**
The Monument c1960
N200002
A little north of the attractive village of Naseby, on the Market Harborough road, this 40 ft high stone obelisk commemorates the Battle of Naseby at which the New Model Army routed the Royalists in 1645, towards the end of the English Civil War. Fairfax's New Model army assembled here before descending to the battlefield. The monument was erected in 1823 by the local lord of the manor.

Road Weedeon c1965 R352015
This view looks south-east towards the much changed crossroads, just beyond the Globe Hotel. The buildings in the distance were demolished to make way for the now much 'improved' and land hungry junction. Most of the shops now offer passing trade antiques rather than haircuts. Note the sign to the then quite new M1 motorway.

Road Weedon, Jan's Folly c1965
R352013
This village is on Watling Street at the junction with the Northampton to Warwick Road. The older village, Lower Weedon, is to the south-west of Watling Street. This view is of the pub, incorporating a lodge. Much enlarged, it still thrives.

Road Weedon The New Inn c1965
R352009
A little uphill from view R352015, The New Inn is set at an angle to the A5 Watling Street and has a 1740 middle with late Victorian wings. It has since been renamed The Heart of England. The old sheet metal and wire workers workshop is now the Chinese take-away, Weedon House.

Newnham, The Village c1955 N251008
Now firmly back in the ironstone hills, we reach Newnham, two miles south of Daventry. The village is set on the hilly north side of the young River Nene. Little has changed. Here we look up School Hill, past New Cottage (new in 1716 when built) to Stone House.

Newnham, The Village c1955 N251010
East of photograph N251008, Frith's photographer looks along Church Street with the 15th-century tower of St Michael's church on the right. Unusually, its lower stage is open and serves as a porch. Beyond is the village hall, a mid 19th century building, now with a concrete tiled roof. A modern stone house now fills the gap between the hall and the stone cottages.

▲ **Newnham, The Romer Arms c1955** N251012
At the west end of the village there is a small green along the Badby Road. The Romer Arms pub is unchanged, but the Daventry Co-op Industrial Society shop (left) has been rebuilt as Newnham Stores and post office. The tree on the right was replanted in the 1980s.

◄ **Upper Boddington, The Post Office c1965**
U51016
Heading south-west towards Banbury, we now reach Upper Boddington, close to the Warwickshire border. This tight-knit village is built along a grid of narrow winding lanes with a fair bit of modern development - but it retains its attractive character. Here we look south along Church Road to the village shop, nestling behind the 17th-century Cobblers Cottage.

◄ **Upper Boddington**
Frog Lane c1965 U51028
Leading north off Warwick Road, Frog Lane is one of most attractive lanes in the village, albeit now interspersed with modern houses of the 1960s onwards. Hillside View, the thatched stone cottage on the left, is unchanged but the one beyond has been dramatically altered so that virtually only the front elevation survives. Beyond this there are now modern houses. The overhead electricity wires and poles remain and the slate roofed house behind, quirkily named Toad Hall. There are more modern houses on the right.

◄ Upper Boddington The Plough c1965

U51017

The Plough pub, now a free house, can be found on the Warwick Road. An 18th century ironstone house with a thatched roof, the outbuilding to the right has been thatched and extended to hide the door (with parcel and the delivered dry cleaning). The brick boundary wall has been rebuilt in stone and is now much lower.

▼ Byfield, High Street c1955

B703004

Just over two miles east of Upper Boddington, Byfield is a village that expanded with the arrival of the railway. This view is on the High Street, part of the A361 Banbury to Daventry road. In the 1950s this was the more minor B4036. Sadly, the long stone range on the left was demolished as a result of road improvement. The bank is now a house, but the Co-op survives as the Co-op Village Store.

◄ Byfield, The Village c1960

B703007

Bell Lane descends to the west of the A361 and gives us a good idea of the variety of building styles that make up this little industrial village. The 1905 primary school is on the left beside the Ford Consul, next to a pair of 1920s brick houses. The pub and hotel at the end has been radically changed and is now Bell Lodge, a residence for the retired and elderly. On the right are 1970s stone-built houses. The road crosses a brook in the middle distance, a tributary of the young River Cherwell.

▼ **Woodford Halse, Moravian Church and Parsons Street c1965** W552004
Woodford Halse grew from a small ironstone village in the later 19th century, partly through ironstone working but mostly when the Great Central Railway arrived in 1899. As a result there are numerous terraces of workers' cottages, all in brick and mainly attached to the west side of the village. This view looks along one of the best streets in Woodford Halse with mainly stone houses and the dominating Moravian Church of 1906.

▼ **Woodford Halse, The Post Office c1965** W552016
Church Street and the roads off to the left are part of a grid of Victorian brick, terraced, straight streets. At the end of the street is the Village Centre, a former school, while to its left you can just see the chancel of the medieval parish church. Woodford Halse Post Office has moved to the electricity shop, while Cundy's, the former post office, is now an empty shop (2002).

▲ **Brackley, Town Hall c1955** B698009
The largest town in south-west Northamptonshire, Brackley had a market charter since before 1217, its wealth having come from wool. The architectural highlight is the Town Hall of 1707, sold to the town by the Earl of Bridgewater for the princely sum of one shilling (5p). Its ground floor was originally open and the clock is dated 1883.

Brackley, The Crown Hotel c1955
B698012

The town is a mix of stone, brick and colour-washed render. One of the best examples of the rendered buildings is the Crown Hotel, which has now expanded to take over Thorpe's the florist to its left. The colour scheme on the Georgian facades is now muted grey with white dressings. The houses beyond all have shopfronts now, instead of domestic windows. The house on the left, behind the Pre-War Austin Big 7, is now an estate agents.

Aynho Park House c1955 A299007
Aynho, on the Oxfordshire border south of Banbury, is a beautiful ironstone village dominated by its great mansion, Aynho Park House. The house was owned by the Cartwright family from 1615 until soon after this view was taken. After uncertain years, the mansion has now been converted into apartments by the Country Houses Association. This view is of the north front, which faces the village, while the south overlooks the River Cherwell valley, across a somewhat mutilated Capability Brown parkland of the 1760s.

Aynho, The Green c1955 A299010
This quiet lane, now the B4100, was a teeming main road until the M40 relieved it of traffic in the early 1990s. Now it is relatively peaceful again. All these stone houses and cottages remain little altered, although the pavement is now smarter. The road has also been widened and has a pavement on the right. This delightful village completes our tour of this most attractive and historic county.

Index

The Francis Frith Collection Titles

www.francisfrith.co.uk

The Francis Frith Collection publishes over 100 new titles each year. A selection of those currently available is listed below. For latest catalogue please contact The Francis Frith Collection **Town Books** 96 pages, approximately 75 photos. **County and Themed Books** 128 pages, approximately 135 photos (unless specified). All titles hardback with laminated case and jacket, except those indicated pb (paperback)

Accrington Old and New
Alderley Edge and Wilmslow
Amersham, Chesham and Rickmansworth
Andover
Around Abergavenny
Around Alton
Aylesbury
Barnstaple
Bedford
Bedfordshire
Berkshire Living Memories
Berkshire PA
Blackpool Pocket Album
Bognor Regis
Bournemouth
Bradford
Bridgend
Bridport
Brighton and Hove
Bristol
Buckinghamshire
Calne Living Memories
Camberley PA
Canterbury Cathedral
Cardiff Old and New
Chatham and the Medway Towns
Chelmsford
Chepstow Then and Now
Cheshire
Cheshire Living Memories
Chester
Chesterfield
Chigwell
Christchurch
Churches of East Cornwall
Clevedon
Clitheroe
Corby Living Memories
Cornish Coast
Cornwall Living Memories
Cotswold Living Memories
Cotswold Pocket Album
Coulsdon, Chipstead and Woodmanstern
County Durham
Cromer, Sheringham and Holt
Dartmoor Pocket Album
Derby
Derbyshire
Derbyshire Living Memories
Devon
Devon Churches
Dorchester

Dorset Coast PA
Dorset Living Memories
Dorset Villages
Down the Dart
Down the Severn
Down the Thames
Dunmow, Thaxted and Finchingfield
Durham
East Anglia PA
East Devon
East Grinstead
Edinburgh
Ely and The Fens
Essex PA
Essex Second Selection
Essex: The London Boroughs
Exeter
Exmoor
Falmouth
Farnborough, Fleet and Aldershot
Folkestone
Frome
Furness and Cartmel Peninsulas
Glamorgan
Glasgow
Glastonbury
Gloucester
Gloucestershire
Greater Manchester
Guildford
Hailsham
Hampshire
Harrogate
Hastings and Bexhill
Haywards Heath Living Memories
Heads of the Valleys
Heart of Lancashire PA
Helston
Herefordshire
Horsham
Humberside PA
Huntingdon, St Neots and St Ives
Hythe, Romney Marsh and Ashford
Ilfracombe
Ipswich PA
Isle of Wight
Isle of Wight Living Memories
King's Lynn
Kingston upon Thames
Lake District PA
Lancashire Living Memories
Lancashire Villages

Available from your local bookshop or from the publisher

The Francis Frith Collection Titles (continued)

Lancaster, Morecombe and Heysham Pocket Album
Leeds PA
Leicester
Leicestershire
Lincolnshire Living Memoires
Lincolnshire Pocket Album
Liverpool and Merseyside
London PA
Ludlow
Maidenhead
Maidstone
Malmesbury
Manchester PA
Marlborough
Matlock
Merseyside Living Memories
Nantwich and Crewe
New Forest
Newbury Living Memories
Newquay to St Ives
North Devon Living Memories
North London
North Wales
North Yorkshire
Northamptonshire
Northumberland
Northwich
Nottingham
Nottinghamshire PA
Oakham
Odiham Then and Now
Oxford Pocket Album
Oxfordshire
Padstow
Pembrokeshire
Penzance
Petersfield Then and Now
Plymouth
Poole and Sandbanks
Preston PA
Ramsgate Old and New
Reading Pocket Album
Redditch Living Memories
Redhill to Reigate
Rhondda Valley Living Mems
Richmond
Ringwood
Rochdale
Romford PA
Salisbury PA
Scotland
Scottish Castles
Sevenoaks and Tonbridge
Sheffield and South Yorkshire PA
Shropshire
Somerset
South Devon Coast
South Devon Living Memories
South East London
Southampton PA
Southend PA

Southport
Southwold to Aldeburgh
Stourbridge Living Memories
Stratford upon Avon
Stroud
Suffolk
Suffolk PA
Surrey Living Memories
Sussex
Sutton
Swanage and Purbeck
Swansea Pocket Album
Swindon Living Memories
Taunton
Teignmouth
Tenby and Saundersfoot
Tiverton
Torbay
Truro
Uppingham
Villages of Kent
Villages of Surrey
Villages of Sussex PA
Wakefield and the Five Towns Living Memories
Warrington
Warwick
Warwickshire PA
Wellingborough Living Memories
Wells
Welsh Castles
West Midlands PA
West Wiltshire Towns
West Yorkshire
Weston-super-Mare
Weymouth
Widnes and Runcorn
Wiltshire Churches
Wiltshire Living memories
Wiltshire PA
Wimborne
Winchester PA
Windermere
Windsor
Wirral
Wokingham and Bracknell
Woodbridge
Worcester
Worcestershire
Worcestershire Living Memories
Wyre Forest
York PA
Yorkshire
Yorkshire Coastal Memories
Yorkshire Dales
Yorkshire Revisited

See Frith books on the internet at www.francisfrith.co.uk

FRITH PRODUCTS & SERVICES

Francis Frith would doubtless be pleased to know that the pioneering publishing venture he started in 1860 still continues today. Over a hundred and forty years later, The Francis Frith Collection continues in the same innovative tradition and is now one of the foremost publishers of vintage photographs in the world. Some of the current activities include:

Interior Decoration

Today Frith's photographs can be seen framed and as giant wall murals in thousands of pubs, restaurants, hotels, banks, retail stores and other public buildings throughout the country. In every case they enhance the unique local atmosphere of the places they depict and provide reminders of gentler days in an increasingly busy and frenetic world.

Product Promotions

Frith products are used by many major companies to promote the sales of their own products or to reinforce their own history and heritage. Frith promotions have been used by Hovis bread, Courage beers, Scots Porage Oats, Colman's mustard, Cadbury's foods, Mellow Birds coffee, Dunhill pipe tobacco, Guinness, and Bulmer's Cider.

Genealogy and Family History

As the interest in family history and roots grows world-wide, more and more people are turning to Frith's photographs of Great Britain for images of the towns, villages and streets where their ancestors lived; and, of course, photographs of the churches and chapels where their ancestors were christened, married and buried are an essential part of every genealogy tree and family album.

Frith Products

All Frith photographs are available Framed or just as Mounted Prints and Posters (size 23 x 16 inches). These may be ordered from the address below. From time to time other products - Address Books, Calendars, Table Mats, etc - are available.

The Internet

Already ninety thousand Frith photographs can be viewed and purchased on the internet through the Frith websites and a myriad of partner sites.

For more detailed information on Frith companies and products, look at these sites:

www.francisfrith.co.uk
www.francisfrith.com
(for North American visitors)

See the complete list of Frith Books at:

www.francisfrith.co.uk

This web site is regularly updated with the latest list of publications from The Francis Frith Collection. If you wish to buy books relating to another part of the country that your local bookshop does not stock, you may purchase on-line.

For further information, trade, or author enquiries please contact us at the address below:
The Francis Frith Collection, Frith's Barn, Teffont, Salisbury, Wiltshire, England SP3 5QP.
Tel: +44 (0)1722 716 376 Fax: +44 (0)1722 716 881 Email: sales@francisfrith.co.uk

See Frith books on the internet at www.francisfrith.co.uk

FREE PRINT OF YOUR CHOICE

Mounted Print
Overall size 14 x 11 inches (355 x 280mm)

Choose any Frith photograph in this book.
Simply complete the Voucher opposite and return it with your remittance for £2.25 (to cover postage and handling) and we will print the photograph of your choice in SEPIA (size 11 x 8 inches) and supply it in a cream mount with a burgundy rule line (overall size 14 x 11 inches).
Please note: photographs with a reference number starting with a "Z" are not Frith photographs and cannot be supplied under this offer.
Offer valid for delivery to one UK address only.

PLUS: Order additional Mounted Prints at HALF PRICE - £7.49 each (normally £14.99)
If you would like to order more Frith prints from this book, possibly as gifts for friends and family, you can buy them at half price (with no additional postage and handling costs).

PLUS: Have your Mounted Prints framed
For an extra £14.95 per print you can have your mounted print(s) framed in an elegant polished wood and gilt moulding, overall size 16 x 13 inches (no additional postage and handling required).

IMPORTANT!

These special prices are only available if you use this form to order . You must use the ORIGINAL VOUCHER on this page (no copies permitted). We can only despatch to one UK address. This offer cannot be combined with any other offer.

Send completed Voucher form to:
The Francis Frith Collection, Frith's Barn, Teffont, Salisbury, Wiltshire SP3 5QP

CHOOSE A PHOTOGRAPH FROM THIS BOOK

Voucher for **FREE** *and Reduced Price Frith Prints*

Please do not photocopy this voucher. Only the original is valid, so please fill it in, cut it out and return it to us with your order.

Picture ref no	Page no	Qty	Mounted @ £7.49	Framed + £14.95	Total Cost £
		1	Free of charge*	£	£
			£7.49	£	£
			£7.49	£	£
			£7.49	£	£
			£7.49	£	£
			£7.49	£	£

Please allow 28 days for delivery. Offer available to one UK address only

* Post & handling	£2.25
Total Order Cost	£

Title of this book . . . .
I enclose a cheque/postal order for £ . . . .
made payable to 'The Francis Frith Collection'

OR please debit my Mastercard / Visa / Maestro / Amex card, details below

Card Number

Issue No (Maestro only)   Valid from (Maestro)

Expires   Signature

Name Mr/Mrs/Ms . . . .

Address . . . .

. . . .

. . . .

ISBN 1-84589-078-7   Valid to 31/12/08

Free Print – see overleaf

Would you like to find out more about Francis Frith?

We have recently recruited some entertaining speakers who are happy to visit local groups, clubs and societies to give an illustrated talk documenting Frith's travels and photographs. If you are a member of such a group and are interested in hosting a presentation, we would love to hear from you.

Our speakers bring with them a small selection of our local town and county books, together with sample prints. They are happy to take orders. A small proportion of the order value is donated to the group who have hosted the presentation. The talks are therefore an excellent way of fundraising for small groups and societies.

Can you help us with information about any of the Frith photographs in this book?

We are gradually compiling an historical record for each of the photographs in the Frith archive. It is always fascinating to find out the names of the people shown in the pictures, as well as insights into the shops, buildings and other features depicted.

If you recognize anyone in the photographs in this book, or if you have information not already included in the author's caption, do let us know. We would love to hear from you, and will try to publish it in future books or articles.

Our production team

Frith books are produced by a small dedicated team at offices in the converted Grade II listed 18th-century barn at Teffont near Salisbury, illustrated above. Most have worked with the Frith Collection for many years. All have in common one quality: they have a passion for the Frith Collection. The team is constantly expanding, but currently includes:

Paul Baron, Jason Buck, John Buck, Ruth Butler, Heather Crisp, David Davies, Louis du Mont, Isobel Hall, Lucy Hart, Julian Hight, Peter Horne, James Kinnear, Karen Kinnear, Tina Leary, Stuart Login, Sue Molloy, Sarah Roberts, Kate Rotondetto, Dean Scource, Eliza Sackett, Terence Sackett, Sandra Sampson, Adrian Sanders, Sandra Sanger, Julia Skinner, Miles Smith, Lewis Taylor, Shelley Tolcher, Lorraine Tuck, Miranda Tunniclisse, David Turner and Ricky Williams.